A
Woman's
Workshop
on
Faith

Books in this series—

After God's Heart:
    A Woman's Workshop on First Samuel
Behold Your God:
    A Woman's Workshop on the Attributes of God
Characters and Kings:
    A Woman's Workshop on the History of Israel
        (Parts 1 and 2)
Designed by God:
    A Woman's Workshop on Wholeness Gifts
Greater Love:
    A Woman's Workshop on Friendship
Growing Godly:
    A Woman's Workshop on Bible Women
Heart Trouble:
    A Woman's Workshop on Christian Character
In Heart and Home:
    A Woman's Workshop on Worship
A Life Styled By God:
    A Woman's Workshop on Spiritual Discipline
        for Weight Control
New Life:
    A Woman's Workshop on Salvation
Open Up Your Life:
    A Woman's Workshop in Christian Hospitality
Our Life Together:
    A Woman's Workshop on Fellowship
People in Turmoil:
    A Woman's Workshop on First Corinthians
Spread the Word:
    A Woman's Workshop on Luke
Talking With God:
    A Woman's Workshop on Prayer
Walking in Wisdom:
    A Woman's Workshop on Eccelesiastes
Your God, My God:
    A Woman's Workshop on Ruth
A Woman's Workshop on the Beatitudes
A Woman's Workshop on Bible Marriages
A Woman's Workshop on David and His Psalms
A Woman's Workshop on Faith
A Woman's Workshop on Forgiveness
A Woman's Workshop on James
A Woman's Workshop on Mastering Motherhood
A Woman's Workshop on Philippians
A Woman's Workshop on Proverbs
A Woman's Workshop on Romans

A Woman's Workshop on Faith

Leader's Manual

Martha Hook

Lamplighter Books
Grand Rapids, Michigan
Zondervan Publishing House

A WOMAN'S WORKSHOP ON FAITH — LEADER'S MANUAL
© 1977 by The Zondervan Corporation
Grand Rapids, Michigan

Lamplighter Books are published by Zondervan
Publishing House, 1415 Lake Drive, S.E.,
Grand Rapids, Michigan 49506

ISBN 0-310-26231-3

Unless otherwise indicated, Old Testament Scripture references are from the *New American Standard Bible,* © 1960, 1972 by The Lockman Foundation, published by Creation House Inc., Carol Stream, Illinois.

All New Testament Scripture quotations are taken from the HOLY BIBLE: NEW INTERNATIONAL VERSION (North American Edition) and copyrighted © 1978 by The International Bible Society. Used by permission of Zondervan Bible Publishers.

Printed in the United States of America

85   86   87   88   89   90   91 / 18   17   16   15   14   13   12   11

To

Dorothy, Alice, Fern, Jo, and Esta,

who asked for the first Workshop on Faith.

OUTLINE OF WORKSHOP

INTRODUCTION

The use of a leader's guide will vary according to the needs of the person using it. In Bible studies today, many men and women are becoming leaders, or teachers, "sharers" of the light that has shone in their lives, who would never wish to teach in a professional sense. They need guides and help, yet not too much complex material. For their sakes, this guide will be simple, yet hopefully adaptable to a wide range of talents.

This guide is meant to be a useful tool in teaching the material involved, but in no way will it substitute for the leader's learning of the biblical material, prayerfully applying it to her own life, then guiding others through the same process. It is doubtful that reversing this process will in any way be successful.

PURPOSE

In describing the purpose of this study, it is necessary to go back to its origin — a small group of women in a neighborhood Bible study. Through the first part of the year, we had studied the Gospel of John. As we were drawn closer to Jesus in the study, we began to realize the inroads He was making into our daily routines. As a result, when the study on John was finished, the women wanted to have some "what-difference-does-it-make-today" lessons.

Together we settled on a list of topics, and the result was this study, A Woman's Workshop on Faith. Through these lessons, we talked openly about how the Bible could shed light on some of life's most common concerns: budget, husbands, friendship, use of time, failure. In each instance, the practicality of the Bible was stressed.

The purpose of studying several women from the Bible was to attract women to a life of faith, to show that biblical women had problems and concerns similar to ours today, and to discover how God worked in their lives to accomplish His purpose.

APPEAL

Too often standards of such excellence are set forth that no one could possibly attain them, nor would anyone *want* to attain them. Above all else, the goal of achieving the life of faith should not be made so lofty as to lose its appeal or practicality. A Women's Workshop on Faith should be explained as an avenue every woman can walk, because every one of us is a special creation of God. It is His desire for everyone to live a life of faith. It is our joy as leaders to see women begin to realize just how much this desire on His part means to them, then to watch how He works in every area of their lives.

HOW TO GET STARTED

There is no sure-fire way to start a Bible study group. It may be as simple as a request from someone that you teach your church circle group, or your Sunday school may decide to do this series of lessons together. If this is your case, you have already begun, and the suggestions below may not be necessary.

For women who do not have an easy situation in which to get started, there are several ways to begin a Bible study. You may want to ask a close circle of friends or your neighbors if they would be interested in this type of activity; or you may get together with one or two friends. At any rate, pray that God will give you the right avenue for your own situation to begin a work for Him. It is usually best if the leader is not the hostess for the class, but you may have to be hostess/leader if you are the only one available.

After you have prayed and determined to begin, arrange a time and a place to get together for the first time. If you are asking women who are receptive to the idea of Bible study from the outset, you may want to announce the time and the topic and plunge right in at the first meeting.

If you ask women whom you do not know well and who may or may not have an interest in a Bible study, it is best to begin with a setting or situation that will give them a chance to understand what you have in mind without overwhelming them with too many things at once. The best way to approach this is to have a coffee or tea for several women at which you can have the materials available and give a brief explanation of what is going to happen in the future Bible study group. You might read or have one of them read the introduction to the lessons and explain that you are interested in investigating this kind of life and would like to invite any who are interested to join you in doing so.

Another approach is to write a letter explaining what you will be doing and send this to people you think will be interested. (And try some you're not sure about!) This approach will give more information, but keep it simple enough for those women who are not used to the idea of a Bible study group.

You will have to choose with God's help the best way to initiate your group. If He wants you to lead a group, He will guide you to the best way and the right women. Be prepared to invite more women than you hope will attend, but do not hesitate to start with a very small group. Also, do not have a big class as your goal. Somehow small numbers lend themselves in a special way to this type of study. You will also find other advantages in small groups — smaller homes may be used for meeting places, and closeness and openness develop more easily with fewer members.

I know of one group that got started from a group of close Christian friends involved in the same business. They got together frequently for social reasons, but always ended up talking "shop" no matter how hard they tried not to. So they began setting aside part of their time together for discussion of a certain topic — then after that time was over, it was usually too late and the conversation too far from business for anyone to want to return to office gossip.

As you can see, there are many ways to begin. Consider which method would work best for you.

SO THEY'RE COMING!

You have been successful in getting a group together — now, how do you get started, and what do you do? Name tags are a must at first if the group is large or if the members do not know each other; and always go on a first-name basis from the beginning, if possible. It is best to keep each lesson time informal and warm. This means you want to avoid a "classroom atmosphere." An atmosphere of love and openness is your first goal.

After a time to get acquainted, your hostess should introduce you, or you may do the honors yourself. With God's help you are the key to this first encounter; and for this reason, it is important to explain who you are, what you do, where you are from, and a few other details of your life, so the women feel they know you and are comfortable with you. From there, you can explain why you believe studying God's approach to womanhood is important. Be sure to make it clear that you are learning too; and that just because you are going to be leading the studies, you are not necessarily an authority on every subject. This is particularly important if you are going to be teaching women who see you in the grocery store with your children who misbehave occasionally! The women who attend the class may want to believe you are perfect, but assure them that you are not before they find out elsewhere.

Either at the beginning or the end of the group time it is good to have a short prayer; but make it simple, not long and impressive. One reason for beginning with prayer is to invoke God's blessing and to lay your time and hearts before Him. Also, hopefully, the class will become close enough to want to pray for one another in the future. If you do have a prayer at some time or another, you have committed the class to God, you have paved the way for praying for one another's needs, and perhaps someday soon, one of them will be able to lead the group in prayer.

"KICKOFF" IDEA

If you need an introductory lesson as a "kickoff" for the series before the serious study begins, ask the women who are present to take a pencil and paper and write down briefly what their impression of the ideal woman is. Ask the women to include in their comments thoughts about career, family, and religion.

Next, have the women share what they have written. It might make it easier to jumble up the papers and hand them out randomly than to call on someone to read her own. From here is the natural bridge into talking about what the Bible has to say about women and their desire for a life of faith. At this point, you may have someone read God's comments on women from Proverbs 31:10-31. Some discussion can be encouraged at this point about how God's description compares with the ones that were read.

Or you may wish to stop with the reading and say simply that the group will find out more about these comparisons when they answer the questions in the first lesson. If you wish to discuss one question in the first class, the first question of lesson 1 lends itself to this purpose, as it requires no outside preparation.

EVANGELISTIC PURPOSE

In this series of lessons, there is a build-up process to the evangelistic lesson, number 4. If yours is a neighborhood class, you will probably have a wide variety of denominations and opinions. By taking three lessons to get to know one another and accustomed to the idea of looking at the Bible objectively, a unity is attained before one is asked to commit herself to the reality of becoming a woman of faith. By the fourth lesson, each woman regardless of her background will be interested in finding how this process would work for her.

After lesson 4 is presented, the following lessons are prepared as if your class were made up of Christians. Obviously, this may not be so. The process of what is involved in becoming a Christian should be gone over many times, both overtly and covertly, so that at each lesson women may open their lives to God. For this reason, a latecomer to the group should be asked to go back and pick up at least one of the first three lessons plus the fourth lesson.

Also, you should remember that the rest of the lessons may be confusing to a woman who does not know Jesus personally. The lessons depend upon letting God work in you, not just "doing" these things in your own strength. If you find someone who is terribly frustrated by these lessons, first be sure you have not made the Christian life seem too lofty, then be sure the woman is operating as a Christian. "You can't live the Christian life without Christ in your life" is a good place to begin a discussion about the individual's need to open her life to Jesus.

SUGGESTIONS

There are some things that will help you as a leader to prepare yourself each week:

1. Study from two modern translations.
2. Set up a schedule of preparation, and then stick to it. It is usually a good practice to prepare well in advance for two reasons:
   a. The material has time to become familiar to you.
   b. Unavoidable last-minute delays will not leave you nervous and unprepared.
3. Set aside a place to keep your materials so they won't get thrown out with yesterday's newspapers.
4. Maintain a prayer concern for each person in your class.
5. Be willing before God to let Him use you.
6. There is much background material available at most community and/or church libraries, so large purchases of research books are not necessary. However, if you intend to be a serious Bible student, beyond purchasing your Bible,

you will probably wish to purchase a Bible commentary, a Bible dictionary, and a Bible handbook.

GENERAL LESSON PLAN

I. Hospitality time	10-15 minutes
II. Prayer time	5 minutes
III. Present need for lesson	5 minutes
IV. Teach lesson with Outline as your guide. The answers to the questions will flow naturally from the teaching process and class discussion.	20 minutes
V. Application and Key Verse	15 minutes
VI. Begin transition to next lesson	5 minutes

Total Time   60-65 minutes

Depending on how well your group responds to doing their assignments at home, you may want to assign some questions as "homework" and reserve some questions to be done in class.

Remember that this manual is only a *guide*. Your own creativity and additions will give the class a special flavor all its own. Glean ideas from magazines, newspapers, radio, and television to use in making your lessons relevant and interesting. Any sort of visual aid adds spark to a lesson. Ask God to help you be creative and adept at presenting this course.

UNIT I: Three Biblical Examples

In this unit some concrete pictures of biblical women will be established. These three pictures will give the now-woman a model off which to bounce her own image. For this reason it is important that the women in your class try to identify with each of these women. From time to time during the series you may wish to refer back to these women to illustrate one of the concepts you are studying. By the time you are finished studying these three women, you should feel that you know them and how they functioned in their homes and cultures. Any way you can think of to make Old Testament women "live" for the women in your class will be helpful.

The purpose in the first lesson is to set up a biblical ideal, while the second two lessons differ somewhat, in that they will show your class two women who are not perfect, yet who function as God's instruments in exciting ways. It is your goal in these lessons to strike a balance between the ideal and reality. Each woman will then be receptive to the fourth lesson during which she can commit her life to God through Jesus — her opportunity to become a woman of faith.

1

A BIBLICAL IDEAL:
"YOU'VE GOT TO BE KIDDING!"

This lesson is fun to lead because women are immediately challenged to do some comparison and self-evaluation. Especially during the first question you should involve the members of the class as much as possible in open and lively discussion. As you go through the passage, steer the women to the verses which apply specifically to the activities of this biblical woman. Since each modern woman has many different talents and interests, your list may become quite long, but each activity that is listed will encourage your class to think of more.

PURPOSE

To see the biblical ideal in comparison with today's woman.

OUTLINE

The verses in Proverbs 31 fall into categories as they relate to various areas of this woman's life. She is seen in various roles, yet always feminine. Below is a verse-by-verse breakdown of all of her relationships.

Self

v. 22 dresses herself well

vv. 17,25 cares for herself, does not fear age

v. 26 is wise and kind

v. 27 is not lazy

Children

v. 21 makes sure her children are cared for

v. 27 is in tune with her family

v. 28 her children love and praise her

Others

v. 14 deals with merchants

v. 16 buys a field if she thinks it wise

vv. 19,20 helps the poor

v. 24 makes a sale-able product

Husband

v. 11 he trusts her; she satisfies him

v. 12 supports and helps him

vv. 13-28 organizes and cares for his home

v. 23 he is well known in the city, a civic leader

vv. 28,29 he praises her

Servants

v. 15 feeds them; organizes them and their time

Activities

vv. 13,19 makes fabrics

vv. 14,15 buys and prepares food

v. 16 plants and tends vineyard

vv. 21,22,24 seamstress

v. 26 speaks with kindness and wisdom

The Result
v. 31 she is blessed and praised

KEY VERSE

"Charm is deceitful and beauty is vain, But a woman who fears the LORD, she shall be praised" (Prov. 31:30).

ANSWERS TO QUESTIONS

1. *List the activities of the woman in Proverbs 31. List your counterpart to each activity.*

   The point of this question is to help the class see that even though we are separated by many years, many miles, and innumerable cultural differences, we are still very much like this woman in our daily routines. We have to cope with many of the same demands she faced. Here are a few suggestions to start with, but your list will vary depending on the talents of the women in your class.

Proverbs 31	Me
1. seeks wool and flax	1. select fabric; shop for good clothing
2. works with hands	2. sew, cook, clean
3. shops for food	3. go to supermarket
4. prepares food for household	4. prepare meals
5. organizes servants	5. give maid work to do and/or make list of things to do myself
6. purchases field	6. buy and sell stock; look for good investments (antiques, collecting, refinishing); hobbies and crafts
7. plants vineyard	7. tend to gardening and yard work

8. makes things to sell	8. find talent that is saleable (Many women have not considered using their talent as a moneymaking possibility.)
9. provides clothing for family	9. mending, sewing, shopping

2. *Are there any areas of life important to you that are omitted from the description in Proverbs 31?*

1) politics	4) medicine	7) travel
2) sports	5) technology	8) entertaining
3) theater	6) education	9) church activities

Obviously, there are differences in our lives today, for few of us live in an Oriental, servant-oriented world any more. Also, there are some areas not discussed in Proverbs. Taking your class's list, see if the activities are hinted at in any way in Proverbs 31. For instance, surely the woman who is the wife of a leader of the city would in some way be interested in politics and entertainment, etc.

3. *From what is said about the woman's husband, how would you describe him? How does he fit the picture of today's husband?*

The imagination can have a good time with the husband in Proverbs, but there are a few definite hints about him:

— is involved in the community
— is highly respected
— loves his wife and family
— is a good provider

This description comes close to what any twenty-year-old girl might say if you asked her to describe what she is looking for in a husband. He is surprisingly like a man today even though he lived thousands of years ago.

4. *What does this woman do for herself? How does she find her self-satisfaction?*

When the Bible says this woman "girds herself with strength," we realize that we do not speak in these terms today. However, she apparently kept herself in good shape physically, something which all of us should be encouraged to do. Also, she sees to it that she is attractively dressed and often makes her own clothing. She finds her satisfaction in life from doing things for others, caring for her family, adding in some way to the family income, and maintaining a good attitude toward life in general.

5. *What basic characteristics underlie the life style of the woman in Proverbs 31? Do these apply to us today or not? If so, how?*

— she fears God
— she takes responsibility
— she is diligent
— she organizes
— she loves her husband and family

These are still the crucial elements of any homemaker — in any culture.

6. *Choose one characteristic from Proverbs 31 that you most want God to develop in you during this course of study.*

Now that the class has compared the woman in the Bible and present-day women, each member is asked to single out a trait she yearns for personally. This can be a time of real sharing in your group. You might divide your class into prayer partners and ask them to pray about this for one another. If your group is not conducive to this type of experience, you might ask each woman to write her desire on a slip of paper for you so that you can pray for her.

APPLICATION

It soon becomes evident that the woman in this passage of Scripture is not some obscure, veiled figure who grinds wheat in a corner of history. She is a vivacious, caring self-starter. She has many desirable qualities. Apart from changing from the age of hand tools to the machine age, she is much like a twentieth-century woman.

Probably someone in your class will say, "But it's impossible to be all of this" — of course it is! The passage of Scripture begins with "Who can find?" this kind of a woman! God drew this picture, and naturally we cannot quite measure up in all areas to this woman and what she represents. This woman is *His* ideal.

At this point, mention that the group will meet some other biblical women with failures and problems, when they study Sarah and Esther. They will feel more comfortable with them.

Some other verses to mention in conclusion are Proverbs 12:4 and 11:16.

2

A BIBLICAL EXAMPLE: "HAVEN'T WE MET BEFORE?"

Now the class moves into the study of Sarah — the mother of the promised son of Abraham. It was through this woman that God chose to bring a race of people onto the face of the earth who continue to influence it even to this day. Why was Sarah chosen? Does she measure up to the woman of Proverbs 31?

For the class to see that God recognizes and chooses to work through our frailties, we will study Sarah in some detail in this lesson. The purpose of this lesson is to balance the idealistic tone of the first lesson, and to set before the women in the class a woman who was not perfect, yet because of her faith and His love, God decided to work in and through her.

PURPOSE

To give a realistic picture of a biblical woman who was considered faithful.

OUTLINE

I. The marriage falters
   A. The couple's deceit (Gen. 12)
   B. Same song, second verse (Gen. 20)

II. The wife falters
   A. Sarah decides to send Hagar to Abraham (Gen. 16:1-4)
   B. Sarah entertains (Gen. 18:1-15)

III. The mother falters
   A. Sarah banishes Hagar (Gen. 16:6)
   B. God deals faithfully with Sarah (Gen. 21:1-8)

IV. Forgiveness for those who falter
   A. Sarah on roll call of faithful (Heb. 11:8-13)
   B. Completeness of forgiveness (Isa. 1:18)

KEY VERSE

"Come now, and let us reason together, says the LORD, Though your sins are as scarlet, they will be as white as snow; though they are red like crimson, they will be like wool" (Isa. 1:18).

ANSWERS TO QUESTIONS

1. *Read the New Testament description of Sarah in Hebrews 11:8-13.*
   a. *How is Sarah described in the passage?* Sarah is listed in the chapter describing God's faithful followers. She had faith that God would do what He said, and through this faith she was able to conceive even though beyond the age of having children.
   b. *How does Sarah compare with the woman in Proverbs 31:30?* In Proverbs 31 it says that a woman who fears the Lord will be praised. In Hebrews, we see the praise of Sarah because she was faithful. She and Abraham are

praised together for their faithful part in helping bring God's chosen people into the world.

2. *Read the Old Testament story of Sarah: Genesis 12; 15–18; 20–23.*

   a. *What was Sarah's faith like?* Somehow Sarah realized that God was leading Abraham, and she followed her husband's leading from Ur. Sometimes Sarah took things into her own hands when she became impatient or didn't understand. This happened when she eavesdropped on the visitors and then laughed when she found out that she was the topic of conversation. Also we see her self-will in sending Hagar in to Abraham. Perhaps this is why she so jealously reacted to protect Isaac from Ishmael. It seems that her feelings about being pregnant when she was old were more from a fear of being a laughingstock than a fear related to lack of faith.

   b. *What was Sarah's life like?* Sarah was the beloved "first wife" of Abraham. She was his constant companion. Everyone knew she was barren. She was extremely beautiful, and even kings of other nations desired her. She cooked for Abraham and his three visitors, so she was also involved in the menial chores of everyday life. When Sarah died, Abraham buried her in a royal tomb in Canaan and mourned deeply for her.

   c. *What was Sarah's attitude toward Abraham?* From all we can tell in this passage, Sarah loved Abraham. She was a silent partner in all he did. They determined beforehand that they would lie about who she was when they went to Egypt and Abimelech. She felt guilty that she was not able to produce the son of promise, so after long periods of waiting, she sent her maid, Hagar, in to Abraham. They have a rather typical argument over

Ishmael, and Abraham reminds her that this was all her idea.

d. *What was Abraham's attitude toward Sarah?* Abraham had known Sarah all of his life and was deeply devoted to her throughout her life both as sister and wife. They shared God's promises together. They had a great feast when Isaac was weaned. There are times when we see them as a couple with problems as well as promises. Abraham followed Sarah's advice about going in to Hagar, and when Sarah wanted to argue about it, he told her make the best out of the problems she had initiated. Again, note Abraham's grief at her death.

3. *List the ways Abraham and Sarah fall short of the moral code of our culture today. Which of these things were moral breakdowns in Abraham's culture?*

    1) Abraham lied about Sarah on two occasions.

    2) Sarah took Hagar to Abraham in order to get a son.

    3) Sarah banished Hagar. This amounted to murder for Hagar and her son because there was no way for the woman and the boy to live.

    4) Sarah eavesdropped when Abraham was entertaining.

    5) Sarah and Abraham were married and were half brother and sister.

The only point at which there were moral consequences in Abraham's culture was when Abraham lied about Sarah. But there were painful consequences to some of the others.

4. *Paint a word-picture of Sarah as if she were living today. Who would she be? Who would her husband be? What would she be like?*

Sarah would probably be the wife of a leader of a nation. Since she is nearby when many things happen, she will sometimes be drawn into questionable activities. She is beautiful and well-groomed, and she is willing to do almost anything for the sake of her husband's career. Sometimes she does things on impulse, and this often causes her great personal conflict. She is embarrassed but proud to become a mother so late in life. She will not hesitate to use her position and power to keep other young men out of the limelight with her child. I think her faith will strengthen in later years when she realizes that her wiles are not necessary for God to work out His plan in her life.

5. *In comparing the accounts of Genesis and Hebrews, Sarah appears to be almost two different women. How can both accounts be accurate?*

   Because of the renewing power of God's forgiveness, Sarah is able to appear on the pages of Hebrews as one of God's faithful ones. She was a woman with problems just like we have today, but when she died, God did not see her with problems, but as forgiven. The memory verse from Isaiah is helpful in seeing how this principle works. As women today we have the same privilege as Sarah.

6. *Briefly describe your pluses and minuses, your good points and your weaknesses. How do you feel about not being perfect? How does God react to your evaluation and your feelings of inadequacy?*

   In this self-evaluation, encourage each woman to include some of her good and bad qualities. Your goal is to help the women see that God does not expect perfection of us any more than He did from Sarah. Explain that you will deal in more detail with this area in lesson 4.

APPLICATION

It is important for the women in your class to see that Sarah is not too different from any of them. She was faced with famine and murder, so she lied. She entertained strangers for dinner, so she eavesdropped on the after-dinner talk. She heard she might have a baby after she was past the childbearing age, so she laughed. She continued childless, so she followed her culture and sent her maid in to Abraham. Later she was fearful that Hagar's son might usurp her son Isaac's place, so she sent Hagar away.

All of these things are perhaps what we would consider wrong. Sarah made some bad choices; she could have done otherwise and chose not to. But God, when He recorded history, did not expect perfection from her, instead He saw her faith (Heb. 11). Endeavor to help your group see that when any woman bounces herself off the mirror of Proverbs 31, she comes up lacking. Sarah comes up lacking, too, but it isn't perfection that God wants. He knows we aren't perfect, and He is willing to deal with us on that basis.

Maybe the life of faith is not what it seems at first. It does not mean being perfect. It does mean reaching out to God in faith and letting Him help you and forgive you; it means allowing Him to help you toward the goals of Proverbs 31.

3

A BIBLICAL HEROINE: "TO BE OR NOT TO BE?"

Like the lesson about Sarah, this lesson about the beautiful young queen of a despot king serves a specific purpose. On any level, women must cope with problems close to home, and Esther is faced with a gigantic problem close to home — a problem that involves her secret identity and her husband's politics. The "hows" and "whys" of solving Esther's problem not only make interesting reading but also give us some womanly know-how for life.

It will be your job as the teacher to know the story well, and to help the women in your class identify with Esther, thus seeing themselves and their situations in a new light. As women, wives, and mothers, we do not always have easy situations in which to live. How can God use us in these situations to accomplish His purpose? How can as simple a thing as a young queen's dinner party play a part in the fate of a nation? Does God ever give us a marriage with dead-end streets in it?

All of these questions will open your class to some lively

discussion. Everyone loves a love story, and almost every woman can identify in some way with Esther and her dilemma, which she cleverly turns into Haman's dilemma. Some mention should be made about cultural differences, but you may wish to keep this factor in the background. The more positive, personal applications should be in the foreground.

PURPOSE

To show how an Old Testament woman in trouble with her marriage remained faithful to God.

OUTLINE

 I. One queen exits (Esth. 1:1-22)
 II. One queen enters (2:1-23)
 III. Haman connives (3:1-15)
 IV. Esther prepares (4:1–5:1)
 V. Esther faces Ahasuerus (5:2–7:10)
 VI. Jews are protected (8:1–10:3)

KEY VERSES

"But the Lord is faithful, and he will strengthen and protect you from the evil one. We have confidence in the Lord that you are doing and will continue to do the things we command. May the Lord direct your hearts into God's love and Christ's perseverance" (2 Thess. 3:3-5).

ANSWERS TO QUESTIONS

1. *Compare Vashti and Esther. How do the two women respond to the varying demands of their culture?*
   Vashti is a woman of principle who refuses to honor her drunken king's request to come to the servants' feast; in doing so, she would leave her own party untended, and she was apparently repulsed by the invitation. Esther is a beautiful woman who does all she can to please the king, but she

is not always pleasing to him (4:4). She is willing to jeopardize her life for her people. Both women are alike in these aspects: 1) Both risk their lives. 2) Both act on convictions very close to their personal feelings. 3) Both are victims of the whims of Ahasuerus.

2. *If you were instructing and preparing Esther, what advice would you give her?*

Do:

    1) Make yourself as beautiful as possible.

    2) Learn all you can about being responsive.

    3) Try to do what pleases the king.

    4) Project an inward beauty.

    5) "Say it"; express verbally your devotion to king.

    6) Be well versed in current things of interest to the king.

    7) Be attentive and affectionate.

Don't:

    1) Reject him.

    2) Be untruthful.

    3) Talk about yourself.

    4) Cross the king unless willing to pay Vashti's price.

    5) Be silly unless he is.

3. *How does Esther accept responsibility with Ahasuerus and for her people?*

Esther does all she can to please the king, and he falls in love with her, even to the point of having a feast in her honor. When she has the crown, she does not hesitate to do all she can to use it for her people. Esther uses flattery, hospitality, and position when it is necessary to save the lives of her people, yet she remains completely feminine — in effect, she wins a war without firing a shot, by being a woman in the right place at the right time.

4. *Describe Esther's reply to Mordecai in 4:16. What does this tell us about her?* Esther agrees to do what she can for the Jews, but she asks for prayer and fasting on her behalf for three days. Fasting has always been an act of devotion. By this response, we see that she has seen what she can do and is willing for God to use her. She responds to Mordecai when he talks about God; she is spiritually responsive.

5. *What kind of strategy does Esther use and what does it tell us about her?* Esther decides to "kill them with kindness" and her beauty. She has always done things to please the king, and she knows that he responds to this sort of treatment. She does whatever she can to help within a bad situation — even though she has not been called to see the king for a month and could have been upset about it. When it became necessary to get the job done, she was ready and willing to do it, and she knew her king well enough to know when it was best to talk — after a good meal.

6. *Why is the story of Esther in the Bible?* This ancient story tells us how God protected the Jewish nation. God had promised them that they would always be special to Him, and that a Savior would come through them. This gives us a glimpse into what the Jews went through as a nation in captivity. It also tells us what one person with conviction and purpose can accomplish when that conviction is toward God. Esther is far from perfect, but her faith colors her entire life style.

7. *List five things you have learned from Esther:*
   1) Prepare yourself for your husband.
   2) Do not hesitate to be "all woman."
   3) Principles are important when crucial issues are at stake.
   4) Do not balk at being one who fits into your husband's life.
   5) Be wholeheartedly pro-husband.

6) Though she was in terrible circumstances, she was able to call upon the Lord with those around her and seek His will in prayer.

8. *Can you see God at work in your situation today? If so, how? If not, what do you wish He would do?* If the women in your group are willing to share some of their feelings about this question, you will have an ideal transition into the next lesson. For the woman who wishes God would do something in her life, but who can't see Him there now, encourage her that this is possible. You may wish to give her some Scripture verses that apply to salvation at this time; but encourage her to study the Scriptures in lesson 4 to see how they apply directly to her dilemma.

APPLICATION

The purpose in studying Esther's life is to give the women of your class another look into the life of a very "human" Old Testament character. Now that they have seen Esther and Sarah, they will be able to see how being a woman of faith is possible not just in theory, but also in life. There are some interesting comparisons of the two women you may want to make. Both women were wives of powerful men, both were desirable for their beauty, both got involved with their husbands' careers, both were in their special positions because God planned to use them in dealing with the nation of Israel.

The main thing for your class to see in Esther is that God is using her where she is; she was not just dumped on the pages of history in a haphazard fashion, but He had her in the palace for a reason. Our lives are the same. Our situations may not be all we could wish for, but God will use us in them.

You will want to prepare your group for the next lesson in a special way. In the next class you will be introducing in detail the concept of how to embark on the life of faith. Therefore, it will be helpful to leave the women with some remarks challenging them to the life of faith. The key verses, 2 Thessalonians 3:3-5, are a bridge from this unit to the next about personal faith. The women have studied both the ideal and practical aspects of womanhood. Now they can make these a part of their own lives. Now these qualities become personal.

UNIT II: PERSONAL FAITH

Unit II is perhaps the most important unit of this study course. Within these two lessons the women of your class will be encouraged to establish their own personal walk with God. You may wish to take more than two class periods with this material if some of the women in your class have never considered these scriptural truths before. At any rate, do not hurry through these times together.

You may find it helpful to have one woman in your class or an outside visitor come and give her testimony about her personal faith before beginning these lessons. If you do this, you will be adding a fourth example to the three women you have studied in Scripture. The personal testimony will make the Bible stories more vivid. Now the women in your class cannot say, "These women were from a different culture. I couldn't possibly walk hand in hand with God."

The purpose of the fourth lesson is to show how to begin the life of faith, and the purpose of the fifth lesson is to find out something about ourselves in relation to Scripture and our self-image.

Remember, with God's help, you are trying to lay a foundation of trust and confidence in God and in His Word. From this juncture, you will go into more details of the Christian life, but from here on, each lesson has this unit as its cornerstone . . . you cannot proceed to the following lessons successfully unless a real relationship with the heavenly Father has been established.

4

YOU AND GOD:
A RECIPE FOR FAITH

From the woman of Proverbs 31, to Sarah, to Esther . . . hopefully by now the women in your class have come face to face with what God expects of a woman, how she can fail, and how she can succeed. All three of these biblical women had faith in God, and their lives were characterized by this faith:

1) "A woman who fears the LORD, she shall be praised" (Prov. 31:30).
2) "By faith Sarah herself received power . . . she considered him faithful who had promised" (Heb. 11:11 RSV).
3) "Go, gather all of the Jews . . . and hold a fast. . . . Then I will go to the king, though it is against the law; and if I perish, I perish" (Esth. 4:16 RSV).

Now that we have these examples before us, the question arises: "How can I have a relationship with God?" Just as God said to Abraham and Sarah that there would be a child of promise but that it would be done in God's way, so He tells us exactly how to establish a relationship with Himself. Make it clear to your group that if we dictate to God how salvation should be accomplished, then we have created a "false God" in our image, not His. To find out God's recipe for faith, we will investigate several passages of Scripture, and by the end of this lesson, each of the members of your group should be encouraged to write their own recipe for faith and put it to use in their own lives.

PURPOSE

To lead the women of the class to a personal faith in Jesus.

OUTLINE

I. God's love for each of us
   A. Tells how God's love motivated Him to send Jesus to protect us from perishing and to give us eternal life (John 3:16)
   B. Jesus loves us with the same love with which God loves Him (John 15:9)
   C. Explains the nature of God's love (Rom. 8:38,39)

II. Our condition as humans
   A. We all fall short of God's standard (Rom. 3:23)
   B. Nothing we do for righteousness is worthwhile in God's sight (Isa. 64:6)
   C. We see what happens when Isaiah comes face to face with God: "Woe is me" (Isa. 6:1-5)
   D. Payment for sin is death (Rom. 6:23)

III. Explanation of what God has done for us
   A. Christ died for our sins . . . and rose again just as the Scriptures said He would (1 Cor. 15:3-6)
   B. Even though we are sinful, God's love sent Jesus to die for us (Rom. 5:8)
   C. Christ's death was final payment for sin; His motivation — to bring us to God (1 Peter 3:18)

IV. Directions for becoming a woman of faith
  A. Open the door of life to Jesus . . . He is waiting (Rev. 3:20)
  B. Belief in Jesus makes us God's child (1 John 5:1)
  C. Salvation is the result of believing in Jesus (Acts 16:31)
  D. This is the day of salvation (2 Cor. 6:2)

V. Description of the benefits in God's plan
  A. Peace with God through Jesus (Rom. 5:1)
  B. No condemnation and freedom from law (Rom. 8:1,2)
  C. Fellowship with others and cleansing from sin (1 John 1:7)
  D. Eternal life is knowing Jesus (John 17:3)

KEY VERSE

"Everyone who believes that Jesus is the Christ is born of God, and everyone who loves the father loves his child as well" (1 John 5:1).

ANSWERS TO QUESTIONS

1. *What is God's attitude toward us?* God loves us supremely. God's love unlike frail, human love is characterized by three things, as seen in these three verses: 1) God's love gives — it is a working love. 2) God's love is seen in Jesus — it is the right kind of love — it is holy. 3) God's love is constant — it is unchanging love. In a day when human love has been elevated and put on a pedestal, it still cannot meet the standards of love which God bestows on us. However, He does not look at our falling short of His standards and react with rejection, anger, or retaliation. He still continues to say, "I love *you.*" This phrase echoes through time down to the present.

2. *What is my situation?* There is nothing I can do to attain

God's righteousness; in fact, my paycheck should be death. Our reaction to our condition can only echo Isaiah's: "Woe is me! for I am lost . . . for my eyes have seen the King, LORD of hosts" (Isa. 6:5 RSV). Even when we do "good things," they do not measure up.

3. *What has already been done about my situation?* Even before we realize our condition before God, He has graciously provided the solution for our dilemma by giving the world the gift of His Son. Our sinful condition does not turn God against us; instead it motivated Him long ago to provide the plan of salvation in Jesus. Jesus paid our price when He died on the cross.

4. *How do I as a now-woman react?* The cornerstone of Christianity is Jesus, and all that is necessary for a life of faith *is* faith — simple belief in what God has done for us through Jesus. There is no "doing" to it: 1) There is "allowing" God to do for us what He has already said He would. If we open the door to our lives, He will come in and live with us there (Rev. 3:20). 2) There is believing in Jesus. This brings salvation and makes us God's child. Just a willingness and an acceptance . . . becoming God's own is that simple, and today is the day some of your class will want to start their life of faith.

At this point in the lesson, it would be wise to say that becoming a Christian is a simple, quiet act of faith before God; however, living as a Christian may not be so simple and quiet. We do not suddenly know the solutions to all of our problems, but now we know and are led by the One who does have the solutions. The rest of this Bible study course will help us learn how to walk hand in hand with God as we live out our new lives with Him.

5. *What difference does all this make in the twentieth century?* The qualities of peace, freedom, fellowship, and eternal life

are priceless. These are qualities which are desirable in any age. They are given in abundance to the Christian, while the rest of the world searches vainly and tries many avenues for the same qualities. Perhaps the way to sum it all up is to say, now we can walk daily with God . . . *just like* Sarah, Esther, and the woman of Proverbs 31!

6. *Compiling the "ingredients" you have just discovered, write your own receipe for faith in Jesus Christ:*

Faith in Jesus   Quantity: Serves the whole world
First, realize God's love. Use liberal amounts; endless supply available.
Mix with the first ingredient:
   1 cup of woe: knowledge of our sinful condition
   1 cup of joy: knowledge of what God has done about our situation
Add slowly while stirring the other mixture constantly:
   1 open heart
   1 full measure of belief in Jesus
Spread evenly over a sinful life
Yield: large batch of eternal life
Bake in the Light of the World (John 8:12) for a lifetime.
Note: Cannot be made in advance and stored.
      Cannot be frozen for use later.
      Why? God's mercies are fresh every day (Lam. 3:23).

APPLICATION

You have covered in some detail the good news about Jesus Christ with the women in your class. This is a great privilege in God's eyes; He has chosen us to be His ambassadors in this world. In order to allow each woman a chance to think about her own condition and relationship to God, do not rush through this lesson. Leave some time for prayerful silence in closing so each woman can establish or renew her relationship with Jesus. Try to be in touch the next few days with any women who do not seem to understand what the implications of this lesson are.

5

YOU AND YOURSELF:
"WHO IS THAT IN THE MIRROR?"

The importance of the preceding lesson cannot be minimized. If today's woman wishes to have a relationship with God like that seen in the first three lessons, she now has the know-how from God's Word upon which to act. From this point on the lessons will deal with topics pertinent to the Christian life; however, the women in your class will not be able to realize the benefits of these lessons unless they act in some way upon lesson 4.

You may wish at this point to visit individually with some of the women in your group in their homes or contact them by telephone. Perhaps some of the other Christians in your class may help in this endeavor. Make yourself available for questions on the part of the nonbeliever. Let the Holy Spirit do the work, but be available to go in whatever direction He leads you to be used by Him in the harvesting of souls.

This is a sensitive area — we do not know at what instant a person establishes a relationship with God. This is up to the individual and God Himself. Pressure from us is not usually the answer — God is His own best salesman. With such a product as eternal life to offer, all we have to do is faithfully present the "good news" and the Holy Spirit takes over from there.

Always keep the "Recipe for Faith" before the class as the starting point for a life of faith; then proceed to enjoy the many facets of the Christian life together.

The first area we will look into is the individual herself. Self-awareness is all-important from the cradle to the grave. Now we will discover that God knows all about our self-image . . . in fact, He created it. He knows all about our fears and anxieties, and in His Word He has given us many insights into His knowledge of our inner needs. Since many of our inner needs are brought on by physical needs, we will also look into some of the physical needs for which God has promised to provide.

We should make it clear that we will not try in this lesson to go heavily into a psychological study of the individual, helpful as this may be; our goal instead will be to look at the Scriptures and their bearing on women of faith.

PURPOSE

To use Scripture as a mirror to find out about ourselves.

OUTLINE

I. Paul's self-image (Phil. 3:4-16)
   A. Paul's personal pedigree of Jewish blood and persever-
      ance (vv. 4-6)
   B. Paul's personal priority list (vv. 7-11)
   C. Paul's personal progress report (vv. 12-16)

II. Our self-image (Matt. 22:37-39)
    A. Proper self-love
    B. Healthy self-love is acceptable in God's eyes

III. Our self-needs satisfied (Ps. 23; Matt. 6:25-34)
   A. David explains God's care for me (Ps. 23)
      1. He is concerned with my physical needs (vv. 1,2)
      2. He is concerned with my spiritual life (vv. 3,4)
      3. He is concerned with my personal fears (vv. 4,5)
      4. He is concerned with the course of my life (v. 6)

   B. Jesus explains the Father's care for me (Matt. 6:25-34)
      1. He is concerned about what I eat: example, the sparrow (vv. 25-27)
      2. He is concerned about what I wear: example, the flowers (vv. 28-30)
      3. He is concerned because He knows what I need (vv. 31-34)
      4. His main concern is His place in my life (v. 33)

IV. God and our self-image (Pss. 139; 37)
   A. God's knowledge of our lives (Ps. 139)
      1. God has complete knowledge of our lives (vv. 1-6)
      2. God is continually with us (vv. 7-12)
      3. God knew us before we were born (vv. 13-18)
      4. David's desire to be completely open before God (vv. 19-24)

   B. Some guidelines for life (Ps. 37)
      1. Trust in the Lord and do good: brings security (v. 3)
      2. Delight in the Lord: brings fulfillment of desires (v. 4)
      3. Commit life to the Lord: brings God's protection (vv. 5,6)
      4. Rest in the Lord: brings contentment (v. 7)

V. Format for a healthy self-image (Phil. 4:4-13)
   A. Joy in circumstances (vv. 4-7)
   B. Changed way of thinking (vv. 8,9)
   C. Leaning on God's strength (vv. 11-13)

KEY VERSES

"Do not be anxious about anything, but in everything, by prayer and petition, with thanksgiving, present your requests to God. And the peace of God, which transcends all understanding, will guard your hearts and your minds in Christ Jesus" (Phil. 4:6,7).

ANSWERS TO QUESTIONS

1. *In Philippians 3:4-16, Paul gives us a look inside himself. After reading these verses, describe Paul and his attitude toward himself (see also Gal. 1:13,14).* Paul had a lengthy Jewish pedigree and every reason to be proud in the earthly sense. But these things were counted as a loss when compared with his spiritual life. He realized that life is more than where you live, who your parents are, what sort of education you have had, and where you go to church. For Paul these things, in comparison with Jesus, quickly fall into the background; in their place is the desire to know Jesus and to share in His life. Notice his comment (3:15) to those "of us who are mature." He realizes that this sort of attitude and desire will not be held by the immature person who may be still wrapped up in his own way of life.

2. *Read Matthew 22:37-39. What does this passage say about you?* Probably the most important verse in the whole lesson, this verse lets us know from the lips of Jesus that we are to love others as we love ourselves. Self-love is implied as a strong and positive force in our lives, worthy of being copied elsewhere in our relationships with others. There is nothing here of self-deprecation or morbid self-denial. When self-love begins to take over other areas of our lives so that we worship self or so that we cannot love others, then it is undesirable; but in the sense of a healthy, positive attitude toward one's self . . . Jesus is all for it. Both Chris-

tianity and psychology agree that our attitude toward ourselves is all-important in our relation to others — if we cannot understand and accept ourselves, we will find it difficult to understand and accept others. We need a self-love that allows us to accept ourselves and others in a healthy way.

3. *Many of our daily activities revolve around concern for our own welfare. Read Psalm 23 and Matthew 6:25-34.*

    a. *What areas of personal need (both material and spiritual) are mentioned in these verses?*

Material:	*Spiritual:*
Food	Peace
Water	Happiness
Safety	Contentment
Clothing	Hope
Moral Behavior	

    b. *What human fears are mentioned in these verses?*

Thirst	Anxiety
Starvation	Exposure
Danger	Uncertainty
Evil	

    c. *How are we supposed to cope with these needs and fears?*

    The way in which we are to cope with these needs and fears is to realize that God is aware of them and that He will supply what we need. The knowledge that everyday needs and fears will be cared for by a loving God allows us to relax and mature in a new way. Our concern is not material, nor is it fearful. Understanding that God knows our earthly needs gives us both comfort and peace. So we do not need to hassle inwardly about these things at all. We need to relax in what God has promised to do.

4. *How is God prepared to help me with my self-image? Read Psalm 139 and Psalm 37:1-7, then write your answer.* Since God knows us totally and can lead us in the way of eternal life, we should not hesitate to trust Him, take delight in Him, and commit our way to Him. Our goal is complete commitment to Him since He knows us inside and out. The more this relationship grows the more our self-image will improve. The confidence of a relationship like this will cause maturity and self-confidence to abound in the life of the believer.

This might be a good time to go back to Revelation 3:21 — we cannot have this sort of relationship and closeness with God unless we have allowed Him to come into our lives. The indwelt life cannot begin without the individual's invitation to God to come in through the open door of her life.

5. *In Philippians 4:4-13, some personal qualities are discussed.*

   a. *From these verses list the qualities you would like to have:*

Joy	Idealism	Peace
Patience	Charity	Excellence
Prayerfulness	Contentment	Purity of mind
		Forbearance

   b. *How can these qualities be obtained by the woman of today?*
      1) Cease worrying and *pray about it.*
      2) Make a conscious effort to *have a changed way of thinking.* Follow Paul's example.
      3) *Be content with whatever our state is:* Our strength is in the Lord, not in our status.

6. *Are there any changes in your self-image that you would like to make? If so, describe how you plan to go about*

making these changes. This question gives an opportunity to apply the principles of the preceding questions to an area of each woman's life. Because we are human, we have the ability to see our failings, and because of God's promises we have the availability of His willingness to change our lives to conform to Him. God is in the business of changing lives, and the more we allow Him to do His work, the more our self-image grows.

APPLICATION

"Beloved, we are God's children now; it does not yet appear what we shall be, but we know that when he appears we shall be like him, for we shall see him as he is" (1 John 3:2 RSV).

The answer to all our needs is wrapped up in God's Son, and we can all look forward to that day when we will see Him as He is. This will be such a powerful experience that it will change us to be all that we have discussed or dreamed of. This is a transforming hope, which can change a dreary self-image to one aglow with expectancy and confidence.

UNIT III: PERSONAL RELATIONSHIPS

After seeing the need for a personal life of faith acceptable to God and to oneself, the women of your class will find a new interest in the basic relationships in their everyday lives. How does this personal faith affect our mates, our families, and our friends?

There are three areas of study in this unit: husband, children, and friends. The Bible has much to say about each of these areas, but selected passages have been chosen to give the women a basis for study. Since you may wish to look at other Scripture passages, you may have to devote more than one study period to each of these lessons. This is especially true of lesson 6.

Keep in mind that it is daily, step-by-step success for which we are working, not something so idealistic it can never be grasped by today's woman. God intended that His principles work in our lives just as they worked centuries ago, so try to make these lessons as practical as possible.

6

YOU AND YOUR HUSBAND:
1 + 1 = 1

In a series such as this, the lesson on marriage is usually a popular one. Whether married or single, we are naturally interested in the subject. We know that God had a special interest in marriage since He likened His relationship with His Son and with us to the marriage relationship.

You will have to be careful to keep your lessons from getting sidetracked onto peripheral issues and problems. First, find out what God and the Scriptures have to say about husbands; then if there is time, try to relate these biblical principles to individual marriages if you wish.

This lesson purposely begins with the Song of Solomon so that a picture of high romance and exotic surroundings opens your study. The reason for this is to encourage frank and open discussion of marriage in all aspects. Just how open and frank this discussion becomes is up to you and your group. The Song of Solomon is a love story. Each marriage in your class has its own love story, so you have a common beginning for this particular study.

From the beginning of meeting and falling in love, each couple must face the possibilities and responsibilities of marriage. These aspects of marriage are studied in detail in the second half of this lesson. In the last part of the lesson, the New Testament passages concerning marriage are discussed. A chart is included that may be helpful in giving an overall picture of what the Scriptures actually say about the issues surrounding marriage.

PURPOSE

To examine the biblical concept of marriage and to allow it to permeate our marriages.

OUTLINE

   I. A biblical love story (Song of Solomon)
- A. Betrothal (1–3:5)
- B. Marriage (3:6–5:1)
- C. Absence and reunion (5:2–8:4)
- D. Discussion of love in marriage (8:5-14)

  II. Paul discusses marriage and life (1 Cor. 7:1-40)
- A. Advice for marriage (vv. 1-16)
- B. Advice for life (vv. 17-24)
- C. Reasons for marital status (vv. 25-36)
- D. Advice for single state (vv. 37-40)

 III. Paul discusses marriage and life further (Eph. 5:15-33)
- A. The Christian life: some instructions (vv. 15-20)
- B. The married life: some instructions (vv. 21-33)

 IV. Peter discusses marriage and life (1 Peter 3:1-9)
- A. Advice for women (3:1-6)
- B. Advice for men (3:7,8)
- C. Advice for life in general (3:8,9)

V. Jesus discusses divorce (Matt. 19:3-12)
   A. God's permanent plan (vv. 3-8)
   B. Why divorce is allowed (vv. 7-9)
   C. Who can accept? (vv. 11,12)

KEY VERSES

"Put me like a seal over your heart, Like a seal on your arm. For love is as strong as death, Jealousy is as severe as Sheol; Its flashes are flashes of fire, The very flame of the LORD. Many waters cannot quench love, Nor will rivers overflow it; If a man were to give all the riches of his house for love, It would be utterly despised" (S. of Sol. 8:6,7).

ANSWERS TO QUESTIONS

1. *Read the Song of Solomon.*
   a. *Describe how love grows between Solomon and his beloved.* Their love grows through days of being together until their statement of complete devotion in the last chapter (8:6,7,10). She is now confident of his love.
   b. *Put 8:6,7 into your own words.* "I want to know that I am in your heart forever. Our love is as strong as death, but jealousy can ruin it. True love can never die, and no money can purchase it."
   c. *What is this couple's attitude toward sex?* They enjoy the sexual side of their marriage thoroughly, and they talk about it openly.
   d. *Why do you think this book is in the Bible?* To show what openness and true intimacy can do for a marriage and to let us know that sex and all of its overtures and expressions are an acceptable part of life. This is not a rubber stamp for any kind of a sex-life on any level, but to encourage a growing intimacy which develops into and throughout marriage.

2. Read 1 Corinthians 7:1-40.
   a. *When and why is it best to be single? What thoughts underlie Paul's logic about remaining single (vv. 8, 25-38)?* It is best to remain single because there is so little time remaining to do God's work. The family man or woman is weighted down with responsibilities and concerns of that relationship. It is essential for those who decide to remain single to have their sexual desires under control.
   b. *When and why should one marry (vv. 1-10)?* When two people are so attracted that they cannot live without one another, they should marry and enjoy it with no guilt.
   c. *What about the marriage of a believer to a nonbeliever?* The believing partner is to stay with the one who does not believe in hopes of winning him or her to Christ. If the nonbeliever leaves, then the believing one is not bound to the marriage.

3. Read Ephesians 5:15-33.
   a. *Why are verses 15-21 a stepping stone to the verses on marriage?* The Christian is to walk happily with God and with others, full of joy and thanksgiving. This passage is a good bridge to the verses about marriage because if one's life is right before God and others, the chances for a happy marriage are greatly increased. It is doubtful that a sad, defeated Christian can have a beautiful, happy marriage.
   b. *What important comparison is made? Why?* The church (body of believers, not just a building) is like the bride of Christ, and marriage is compared to this simile. The same selfless, loving attitude as Christ has for His church should permeate a marriage.
   c. *Comment on the biblical concept of order in the home.* On the basis of the illustration of the church and Christ, wives should submit to their husbands' leadership.

Husbands should love their wives as Christ loved the church, as if the wife is a part of her husband's own body. There are three directives here: the husband is to love, and the wife is to respect, but both are to submit to each other.

   d. *What three commands are given in these verses?* 1) Live in harmony. 2) Wives submit to husbands. 3) Husbands love wives. These three commands, coupled with the concepts of a vibrant spiritual (15-21) life, are the four corners of a happy marriage. Without any one of the four, the marriage will tilt dangerously when pressured, allowing the contents of the marriage to spill over, or inviting an outside force to fill the need for support in some area.

4. *Read 1 Peter 3:1-9.*

   a. *Describe the concept of "submission."* Submission is an adaptation to the husband's needs, a fitting in with a husband's plans and life style. It means an equal partnership in life together, but a reliance upon the husband as the leader of the home.

   b. *What is the biblical concept of "adorning"?* Adornment for the Christian wife should be "inner," not clothing and jewelry, but qualities of life, refinement of spirit, and attitudes of a quiet contentment. Often these qualities will so enhance a woman's physical appearance that she will be far more beautiful than if she spent great effort in dressing herself. All the powers of the cosmetic industry are at a loss to improve an unhappy countenance.

   c. *How is Sarah an example? (Refer to lesson 2 in the light of this passage.)* Sarah was willing to go anywhere and do anything with Abraham. She left the security of home and friends when Abraham decided to follow God's command to move to another land. She cooperated in his schemes to protect their lives by jeopardizing herself with two men. She trusted God for the future, and even though she faltered at times (as in the incident with Hagar), she finally lived to see how God could bring His promise to light without her help.

d. *What does verse 7 say about togetherness in our now-world?* We receive God's blessings as partners. God blesses when we are living in a happy balance together.

5. *Read Jesus' comments on marriage and divorce in Matthew 19:3-12 and put in your own words what He said. How do you feel about this subject?* This question is to encourage the women in your class to think through the divorce issue and to sort out their own thoughts on the subject. You will probably have a lively and perhaps heated discussion at this point, so be prepared and thorough with your own answers. The key to what Jesus is saying is found in His statement, "Let anyone who can, accept my statement," and in the fact that this is a trick question on the part of the Pharisees which He beautifully turns around, and in so doing leaves them speechless.

6. *List what you think are the five most important elements in marriage today.* Love, respect, order, faith, affection, (partnership, trust, forgiveness, acceptance, generosity, companionship, communication); your list of different answers may be endless, but encourage your students to be as open as possible about this question.

a. *Do these balance with what you have learned from the Bible?*

b. *Are these elements found in your marriage? If not, write out how you would like to go about incorporating them in your home and marriage.* Encourage the women to share one change they would like to see in their marriages and to pray for one another if your group is conducive to this by now.

APPLICATION

Often women do not realize that the Bible speaks so openly and practically about marriage. Just discovering the biblical principles is often enough to straighten out a situation causing stress in a marriage.

Perhaps the most important thing modern-day psychology has shown us about marriage (although Solomon also alludes to it) is that good communication is of utmost importance if a marriage is to grow and develop. Some good discussion can take place in your class about how to communicate.

Our society tells us if we look pretty, smell good, eat well, and dress right, we will keep our husbands happy. Thankfully, the Bible goes beyond these surface things and gives us some principles about how to relate to our husbands and their needs.

7

YOU AND YOUR CHILDREN: "GOD BLESS THEM"

If there were any foolproof method of rearing children, surely we would know about it in our computerized world. Even though countless men and women from every culture have been parents, no one has been able to say that they have found the one and only way to care for a family.

Perhaps the strongest reason for our inability to set clear patterns for parenthood is the children themselves. By nature, children rebel at being pushed one by one through the same process. From earliest childhood, the child struggles to be an individual. It is no wonder that the woman of today must give herself uniquely to each of her children.

We realize when confronted with the delinquency statistics that unless we are relatively successful in this area, we are only helping our children to carve out a life of misery and uselessness for themselves. Our dilemma: there is no way to learn how to become a parent but to be one!

But there are numerous references in the Bible to the family, so we will examine several of these to give us some "handles" on parenthood from God's perspective. Our goal is to become parents who walk by faith and who trust God for wisdom at every turn in the road.

PURPOSE

To become mothers who walk by faith.

OUTLINE

I.   Parental petition and problems (1 Sam. 1-3)
     A.   Hannah
     B.   Eli's sons
     C.   Samuel

II. Parental relationships
     A.   Command to honor parents (Exod. 20:12)
     B.   Disrespect of parents (Prov. 30:11,17)
     C.   Reminder to children and parents (Eph. 6:1-4)

III. Parental advice (Prov. 1–10)
     A.   Solomon's ideal for young men
     B.   Solomon's instructions to young men
     C.   Reward for following Solomon's advice

IV. Parental commands (Deut. 6:4-9,20-25)
     A.   The first commandments (6:4-9)
     B.   Explain the commands to children (6:20-25)

KEY VERSES

"Hear, my son, and accept my sayings, And the years of your life will be many. I have directed you in the way of wisdom; I have led you in upright paths" (Prov. 4:10,11).

ANSWERS TO QUESTIONS

1. *Read the story of Samuel and Hannah in 1 Samuel 1–3.*
   a. *Explain Hannah's attitude.* Hannah was upset because

Peninnah had children and she did not. Hannah's method of handling her disappointment was to pray about it diligently and trust God for the answer.

b. *What was the difference between Eli's sons and Samuel (2:12,26)?* Eli's sons did not love God and they cheated on the sacrifices brought to the temple. However, Samuel grew in wisdom with God and man.

c. *How did God honor Hannah's dedication (1 Sam. 7:12-17; 8:1-9)?* Samuel grew to be a man of God. God blessed Israel during Samuel's life, and He used Samuel in mighty ways to reach Israel for Himself.

d. *What have you learned from Hannah?* Hannah faced her predicament with prayer. She made a vow to God, and she kept it. She continued to show her love to Samuel by bringing him clothing. Because she was faithful with one child, God trusted her with several more children. We as women of faith should not fear to trust God with our children, no matter how small the problem or crisis. Hannah so trusted God that she was willing to leave Samuel in what must have been less than perfect conditions for a child. It is interesting that God did not seem to establish any sort of pattern of leaving children at the temple since the rest of Hannah and Elkanah's children were not conceived under the same sort of conditions as was Samuel.

e. *What was the difference between Hannah and Eli?* Hannah was above all a mother, and Eli was above all a priest rather than a father.

2. *What key to parenthood is found in these verses (Exod. 20:12; Prov. 30:11,17; Eph. 6:1-4)?* All of these passages speak of honoring and respecting parents, and such responses will even lengthen one's life span. But the crucial idea is up to the parents, not the children. They must live so

that they deserve respect and so that they do not provoke their children into angry reactions. Respect cannot be forced, rather it grows out of a relationship.

3. *Read Proverbs 1–10. What can we learn about child-rearing from King Solomon?* There is no one right answer to this question since the passage is lengthy and the suggestions are innumerable. There are several underlying concepts which we are looking for here. 1) Solomon covers almost every aspect of life with his counsel. 2) He obviously had convictions of his own which he was not hesitant to pass on to the young men around him. 3) He continually praises the virtues of wisdom, for he knows that if the young man has wisdom he will automatically have many other qualities mentioned in Proverbs.

   Solomon's wisdom is contemporary. The issues that concern this ancient king are the same issues that face our society — free love, wise investments, politics, and so on. The problems that concern fathers and sons today are simply part of being human; these are the crucial areas of concern no matter when a person lives. Your class may want to pick out one or two areas of current interest in your community and discuss what the "wise" solution to these might be.

4. *What were the Israelites commanded about their children in Deuteronomy 6:4-25?* The Israelites were commanded to teach their children the commandments as they were given to Moses. These are not just "adults only" rules, but guides for life no matter how old or young the person is. The commandments are to be so much a part of daily life that it will be natural to talk about them as you work or live side by side.

   The second part of the commandment concerns answering the questions of your children. Whenever an opportunity is given, parents should share what God has done in the past with the children of the present day.

5. *Does the Bible give us any examples of a "perfect" family?* No! Not even Jesus' family. There are countless stories of families in the Scriptures, but none is perfect . . . not David's, not Adam's, not Saul's, not yours, and not mine. Families have problems because people are not perfect, and we need to look for God's guidance daily for our families.

6. *Write down your greatest need as a parent and be ready to share it.* This question will put two mothers in touch with one another in a private situation. Stress the need for respecting the confidence of the other person. Encourage the women to pray together and look to Scripture for their answers. Be available to help if necessary on this question, as some women may need direction about Scripture passages.

APPLICATION

Even though we realize we will never be perfect parents, now we have some insight into God's outlook on the family. In every passage, the burden of proof falls back on the parent, who must take the responsibility for establishing a home and parental situation that pleases God. Through Hannah we see that God understood her desire for a family and responded to her prayerful attitude. Through Solomon we see how God pours love and concern through us to our sons and daughters. In Exodus and Deuteronomy we see the need for discipline and teaching, which grow out of an atmosphere of love and respect in the home.

With the home failing so drastically in our society today, we need to stress the validity of the claims of Scripture in this area. This is a time when the experienced mothers in your class can reach out with love and concern to the mothers who are having problems with their children. As the leader, you should try to pair up women who could be of help to one another. Encourage the pairs to stay in touch with each other.

A Christian home can and should be a positive and happy experience for both children and parents.

8

YOU AND YOUR FRIENDS:
DOUBLE THE JOY AND DIVIDE THE LOAD

We live in a world of lonely people. Even with more people in the world than ever before, people complain of loneliness and lack of companionship. At the heart of Christianity is love for others, so we as Christian women have a unique outlet in meeting this need in the lives of lonely people. All too often we are attracted to people who like people — those who are affable and open; however, it is the lonely, scared, often rejected people to whom Jesus opens a whole new realm of relationships. In His message of acceptance and love is the basis for the beginning of new friendships and companionships.

If your need is companionship, Jesus has promised to walk with you; if your friend's need is companionship, perhaps in God's plan you are the answer. If we allow ourselves to be open to the people that God puts in our path, not just the comfortable friendships of the life we now lead, we may find a whole new world of new friends awaiting us. God knows that we need other believers to walk with and He rarely leaves us without a friend for very long.

In your class you will no doubt find some women who are searching for real companionship, so do not let this opportunity slip by without befriending some new person in the class. All of our talents as hostesses can be put to use in this area, but the one-to-one get-together is often the nicest way of all to make a new and lasting friendship.

PURPOSE

To so fit into the body of Christ that we function well in relationship to others.

OUTLINE

I.   The essence of friendship (1 Cor. 12,13)
   A. Spiritual gifts are given to true believers (12:1-3)
   B. Spiritual gifts may differ but are all given by the same Spirit (12:4-11)
   C. Spiritual gifts function like a body (12:12-31)
   D. Spiritual gifts without love are useless (13:1-13)

II. An example of friendship (1 Sam. 17:55– 20:42)
   A. The relationship between Saul, Jonathan, and David (17:55–18:4)
   B. Saul's inability to cope with David's success (18:5-9)
   C. Saul's attempts to murder David (18:10–19:12)
   D. David's friends (19:12–20:42)

III. The exercise of friendship (1 Thess. 5:14,15; 2 Thess. 3:13-15)
   A. How to react to the difficult friendship (1 Thess. 5:14; 2 Thess. 3:14)
   B. How to react to evil from others (1 Thess. 5:15; 2 Thess. 3:15)

KEY VERSES

"There are different kinds of working, but the same God works all of them in all men. Now to each man the manifestation of the Spirit is given for the common good" (1 Cor. 12:6,7).

ANSWERS TO QUESTIONS

1. *Read 1 Corinthians 12.*
   a. *What is the common denominator of all that we do (vv. 4-7)?* The Holy Spirit is the source of all our various abilities. He places us in the body of Christ and gives us a function there.
   b. *Why are we all different (v. 11)?* The Holy Spirit has given each one of us different functions because there are many different areas of service to be filled. We cannot all do the same thing at the same time.
   c. *What comparison is made (vv. 12-26)?* The interrelated nature of the use of spiritual gifts and the dependence of the human body upon its components are compared. Our physical bodies have many parts, and in the same sense there are many kinds of gifted Christians. The key to the comparison is the interdependence of all the parts of the body. The hand needs the eye, the tongue needs the brain, the blood needs the lungs. And in the same way, the body of believers needs people of differing talents and gifts.
   d. *What happens when a Christian suffers (vv. 22-26)?* The painful experience of one believer, whether an inner conflict or a physical problem, should bring concern and suffering to all of us by nature of our close union in the body of believers.

2. *Read 1 Corinthians 13.*
   a. *What is better than any of the gifts mentioned in 1*

Corinthians 12? The gift of love is to be prized above any of the other gifts, for without it, the other gifts are relatively useless. In fact, they become bothersome like a clanging bell, just so much loud noise.

b. *What gifts are considered worthless without love (vv. 1-3)?* Some of the gifts that men, religious men, consider most important are the ones included in this list: prophecy, faith, martyrdom, tongues. This list and the motivation for our "good acts" should always be under scrutiny for this reason. Our formula is: No love = no good.

c. *What is uncharacteristic of love (vv. 4-8)?* Love will never be jealous, envious, boastful, proud, haughty, selfish, rude, demanding of its own way, irritable, touchy, a holder of grudges, or critical.

d. *How long will love last (vv. 8-10)?* All of the other gifts will pass away because they are not complete and they fluctuate with our situations (age, temperament, health, etc.), but love will continue forever. It is one of the three undying principles: faith, hope, and love.

3. *Read the story of Jonathan and David in 1 Samuel 17:55–20:42 and 2 Samuel 9.*

a. *What did Jonathan do for David?* Jonathan loved his friend, David, so much that he saved David's life and went against his father in doing so. Jonathan still continued to love Saul, but he reacted to the evil that Saul was determined to do. Jonathan, the rightful heir, helped David, even though he realized that David would be the next king. Throughout the friendship, Jonathan was motivated by love; Saul, in contrast, was eaten up with jealousy. It is an interesting picture of two men given the same information, who because of their contrasting motivations have completely different reactions.

b. *What kept Jonathan from jealousy like Saul's?* Jonathan

acted on the basis of a love relationship between David and himself, and he never faltered from that attitude. His love kept him from jealousy and revenge. This also indicates that Jonathan must have had a deep conviction about Samuel's prophecy concerning David.

c. *What prompted David's action in 2 Samuel 9?* David's concern for Mephibosheth goes back to the original love that he had for Mephibosheth's father, Jonathan. Also, David made a promise to Saul (1 Sam. 24:21) which he kept when he was kind to Saul's grandson. Because he was still able to love, he was able to help Mephibosheth.

4. *Obviously we do not get along perfectly with everyone. When this happens we often brush it off as a personality conflict. What can we do today about these situations? Give your answer after reading 1 Thessalonians 5:14,15 and 2 Thessalonians 3:13-15.* In these Scripture passages we are given a foolproof formula for friendship if done in love! We are to encourage, comfort, care for, and be patient with those around us. However, if we do find a Christian who is at fault, we are not to be drawn into his problem, and, we are to help him as a brother to find a solution to his problem. There are very few conflicts that cannot be resolved by applying this simple two-way formula.

5. *What is the basis and evidence for your three closest friendships? What have you learned to help you deepen these friendships?* The reason for these questions is to give each woman an opportunity to check into her friendships. Often our relationships with others are shallow and unproductive; however, by gaining new perspectives about friendship in the Scripture, these shallow friendships can grow into relationships of true concern and love for one another. This lesson should give each woman several new ways to deepen her present friendships and to make new ones.

APPLICATION

Now that your class has looked at what the Bible has to say about friendships, they should be ready to develop friends in a new way. You will want to encourage them to learn to do things for others without expecting anything in return; to accept their friends with an open, noncompetitive attitude; and to let love and interest rather than social standing determine whom they reach out to.

Challenge each woman to make a new friend in the next week and apply these principles to the friendship. So often the woman who suffers from loneliness has mostly herself to blame. As Christian women we should freely take the initiative to make new friends and to minister to the needs of our long-term friends.

UNIT IV: LIFE'S COMMODITIES

Everyone has the same number of hours in the day, but few people spend them in the same way. Everyone has a different amount of money, and it also can be used in myriad ways. Too often the misuse of these two commodities of life — time and money — jeopardizes the happiness of other areas of life. If a mother is frustrated over her confused schedule, it is small wonder she cannot muster up the patience to deal with a child's inappropriate behavior while she is trying to cook dinner. If a wife has not managed her budget properly, she may find it difficult to accept her husband's reactions toward her at the end of the month when there is no money left for groceries.

None of us will ever have enough time or money if we apply the principles of selfish human nature to our desires. We always seem to need more time and more money. And there are hundreds of books available to one who wishes to pursue the world's ways of gaining more of each.

Our purpose in this unit will be to examine the wisdom of the Scriptures as it applies to godly women of faith wanting God's insights into these areas of their lives. For this unit to be successful, it must go beyond the group meeting into the world in which the women live, and it must be practical. Encourage each woman to be willing to make the changes necessary to put the biblical principles into action daily with her calendar and pocketbook. God gives us great freedom in the areas of time and money, but that freedom can allow us to become slaves to those things unless we follow the Lord's principles.

9

YOU AND YOUR TIME:
NEVER SAY NEVER

In looking at ourselves as women of a time-oriented society, we need God's help in organizing and planning our time. If we do not plan certain activities into our schedule, our time is rapidly wasted away in the humdrum activities of living. On the other side of the issue, since so much of our time is spent in the mundane, it would make sense that we examine our lives to be sure that we richly enjoy every minute of our lives, not just the fun-filled, special times.

First and foremost, we need to be sure that we are using our time wisely — especially that part of our time in which we do most of our living. Are we too involved in any one area? Are we resting enough? Are we trying to do too many things in one day? Any one of these things can tip the balance between contentment and frustration.

In this lesson we find that God directs all of time itself, so in reality, we have very little control over time. Actually, time can control us much more easily than we can control it. We have only a few minutes in a day which are not directed by responsibility, and we have no minutes in a day which are not under God's direction.

PURPOSE

To realize that giving God control of our calendar releases us from its control over our lives.

OUTLINE

I. Self-evaluation of time
   A. Our activities
   B. Our relationships

II. Control of time (Luke 12:19,20; Acts 1:7; James 4:13,14)
   A. God's power: control of history, tomorrow, death
   B. Our dilemma: no control of history, tomorrow, death

III. God's view of time (2 Peter 3:8; Rev. 21:6)
   A. A different time-style
   B. Man's boundaries

IV. Use of time (2 Thess. 3:6-16)
   A. Occupation
   B. Spare time

V. Reason for time (Eccl. 3:1-15)
   A. Man's realization and frustration
   B. God's control gives freedom from frustration

VI. Wise planning about time (Matt. 6:33,34; Eph. 5:15-17)
   A. Good use of time
   B. Allow God's control of time

KEY VERSE

"He said to me: 'It is done. I am the Alpha and the Omega, the Beginning and the End. To him who is thirsty I will give

to drink without cost from the spring of the water of life' ''
(Rev. 21:6).

ANSWERS TO QUESTIONS

1. *Give a time outline of how you spend a typical day.* This
   question is meant to draw attention to how much of our
   time is spent in just functioning — dressing, cleaning, eat-
   ing, sleeping. All too often we do not want to think these
   things are worthwhile, yet here we see it in black and white:
   just living takes up most of our time.

2. *Estimate your time spent daily with the following on a
   percentage basis: (a) friends, (b) relatives, (c) children, (d)
   husband, (e) yourself, (f) God.* In answering this question
   we find that our time is activity-oriented rather than
   people-oriented. We say we care about others, but actually
   we find that very few minutes are spent with people. There
   is a trick to this question because in both ''e'' and ''f'' the
   answer is 100 percent. We are never apart from ourselves
   or from God, so we need to be doubly sure that we have a
   positive attitude about ourselves and about our relationship
   with God. Here is a good point at which to review some
   facts from lessons 4 and 5 about self-image and our relationship with God.

3. *Over how much time do we exercise ultimate control? Use
   the above questions for reference, and also read Acts 1:7;
   James 4:13,14; and Luke 12:19,20.* The obvious answer is
   ''Very little.'' Acts 1:7 tells us that God has set times and
   dates for history. This power is part of God's authority over
   the universe. James 4:13,14 explains that people think they
   control time and what they do with it; however, deep inside
   everyone knows that the future is an unknown to humans.
   Luke 12:19,20 explains that people think that storehousing
   riches will protect them from the future. But God says when

our life shall end, so He is the one who holds our lives in His control. In short, we do not control times in history, we do not control tomorrow, and we do not control how long we shall live.

4. *Is God's view of time the same as ours? Refer to 2 Peter 3:8 and Revelation 21:6.* The idea that God does not have to wind His watch has never occurred to many people. Because of the anthropomorphism in so much of our thinking, we tend to think that God is locked into time in the same way creation is. However, in these verses we see that God is free from any sort of time in the same sense that we understand it. He knows and understands time, but it does not rule over Him as it does us. He operates outside of time, while our humanity keeps us closely tied to it.

5. *What kind of use of time does Paul recommend in 2 Thessalonians 3:6-16?* Each person is to work for his own living and to care for his own affairs. His three points are: 1) quiet down, 2) work, and 3) earn your own living.

6. *What key to spare time does 2 Thessalonians 3:13 give us?* "Never tire of doing what is right." This is our guide. If we are involved with others and working as we should, it is doubtful that there will be much time left over. This thought should cause us to examine our activities to be sure they are not just "calendar fillers," but that they have a purpose that is directed by this verse. It might be interesting for your class to think back on the woman of Proverbs 31 to see if she has activities for her spare time.

Another aspect enters in here. Each of your women should be challenged at some point during the course to establish her own time alone with God. This time is essential to growing in the Christian life. Some helpful guidelines here may help your women to begin a rewarding life of walking daily with God.

7. *Why did God give us time and put us in a time-oriented environment? Read Ecclesiastes 3:1-15.* The purpose in giving us time is to show us our humanity. We cannot know the end from the beginning. God did this so that we would reverence Him when we realize His ultimate control. Man's frustration with time is meant to point him to God. This is the key that frees many women from frustration over lack of time; on the basis of this premise, when frustration comes over us, we are able to thank God for it, realize again our humanity, and recognize our need for Him. If this answer does not bring a huge sigh of relief from your group, go back over it!

8. *Now that you as a busy woman understand these concepts about time, what difference will it make in your daily routine? Read Ephesians 5:15-17 and Matthew 6:33,34.* This is a summary question to encourage your group to take a positive approach to their schedules. Now that they know God is in control of their time, they should be encouraged to work with Him and His principles in setting up a workable routine. Some hints about organizing time and work, the setting up of priorities in their schedules, and even the simple guideline of making out lists will be helpful to most of the women.

APPLICATION

The release from worry and frustration about time is truly one of God's most gracious gifts, but it can only be realized as we apply God's principles, not ours, to our life styles. There is nothing wrong with being organized, in fact it is a most desirable quality; however, we can never depend upon our ability to organize to make us feel fulfilled at the end of the day. Only the woman who has sat down and prayed about her schedule with God's principles in mind will be able to see what is best for her to do with her time. Since only God knows the end from the beginning, it should encourage us to walk closely with Him. Our frustration with our busy lives and schedules is really only God's gentle reminder to us to let Him have the control of our time.

10

YOU AND YOUR BUDGET:
HOW MUCH IS ENOUGH?

Many of the joys and problems of the present age are linked to our having or not having material wealth. The most highly regarded measuring stick throughout most of the world is the current price of gold, and in many of our homes and pocketbooks it also reigns supreme. For centuries men have searched for hidden treasure, wealth in faraway lands, formulas to make gold, and a quick, bullish turn in the stock market. The secular world realizes the thumbscrew that materialism can be. "Our possessions are worthwhile only if they enhance our lives. When the things we own start to own us; when they turn us into slaves; when they get in the way of human relationships and drain us of time and money — then it's time to ask whether they're worthwhile."[*]

If our faith is to help us in the area of personal budgeting we

---

[*] Myles Cullum, "Materialism, a Threat to Family Life," *Better Homes and Gardens* (November 1973): 4.

must have clear biblical guidelines on which to open or shut our purses, and when to sign or not sign a charge slip. God has not left us in the dark when it comes to this part of our lives. Many of Christ's comments and parables apply to us and our bent toward materialism. In your introduction to this lesson you might ask your class to suggest all of the passages in the Bible they can think of that talk about money. The list is long: the Sermon on the Mount, the widow's mite, the prodigal son, the lost coin, and so on. The list is surprisingly extensive, so take advantage of the discussion time.

Women today probably control a higher percentage of the world's money than ever before, so we should be careful as women of faith who wish to please God to prepare ourselves for this responsibility. The questions and answers in this lesson are not difficult or extensive, but the application of the material may take years and years of trial and error. Of utmost importance is learning to see our budget as a means of serving God. He should be in control of all of our money, not just a percentage; then we can use it as He directs.

PURPOSE

To allow God's Word through faith to determine our budget criteria.

OUTLINE

I. Riches: ownership and priorities
   A. All belongs to God (Ps. 24:1; 50:10; 1 Cor. 10:26)
   B. The foolish man's priorities (Luke 12:13-21)
   C. The spiritual man's priorities (Luke 12:22-39)

II. Riches: examples and principles
   A. Solomon (1 Kings 3:3-15)
   B. Ananias and Sapphira (Acts 4:32–5:11)

III. Riches: give and take

A. Talk to God about needs (Matt. 7:7-11)
B. Give freely from what God gives us (Phil. 4:10-20; 1 Cor. 16:2)

KEY VERSE

"And God is able to make all grace abound to you, so that in all things at all times, having all that you need, you will abound in every good work" (2 Cor. 9:8).

ANSWERS TO QUESTIONS

1. *How much of our world belongs to God? Read Psalms 24:1; 50:10; 1 Corinthians 10:26.*
   a. All the cattle, mountains, and the world belong to Him.
   b. The earth belongs to God.
   c. All these belong to God and are ours to enjoy.

2. *Read Luke 12:13-40.*
   a. *How many basic principles for today's woman and her money can you find in this passage?*
      1) Man is more valuable to God than a flock of sparrows (v. 6).
      2) Do not always be wishing for what you don't have (v. 13).
      3) Real living is not related to riches (v. 15).
      4) It does no good to worry about material things (v. 22).
      5) God will provide what we need (vv. 24-28).
      6) Give to others (v. 33).
      7) Be ready for the Lord (v. 40).
   b. *Briefly tell the story of the man in verses 16-21. Why is he called a fool?* The man built barns and filled them, then trusted in them for future provision. He did not know he would die that night, but God did. He is called a fool because he failed to realize that his soul was more

important than his riches, and he never understood the fact that his life was in God's hands.

c. *For what are we always to be prepared? How can we prepare ourselves for this event?* We are always to be ready for the Lord's return. We can only prepare ourselves through personal faith, by keeping confession and forgiveness in operation, and by keeping the communications open between us and the One who is coming.

3. *How does the story of Solomon (1 Kings 3:3-15) compare with the story of the rich farmer in Luke 12?* Solomon asked for wisdom and God gave him riches as well because Solomon would use them wisely. Instead of storing up and depending on riches, he knew he needed wisdom to deal with what he had. God expects us to deal with our riches with wisdom and by operating on His principles, not the world's. It is interesting to notice that God increased Solomon's wealth; therefore, we know He can bring great wealth to His children. His pleasure comes when His children look for His guidelines in using the wealth.

4. *Read Acts 4:32–5:11.*

a. *Describe the financial situation in the young church in Acts.* Everyone helped those in need by selling what they had and by giving it to other less fortunate Christians.

b. *What was the sin of Ananias and Sapphira?* Their sin was not in having too many riches but in lying and trying to deceive. They wanted the praise and the pocketbook too.

5. *How do we balance what we need and what we give? Read Matthew 7:7-11; Philippians 4:10-20; 1 Corinthians 16:2.* According to Jesus' teaching, we are to feel free to ask God for what we need, and expect that He will answer us

lovingly. At this point it might be wise to back up and read a few verses in Matthew 6 about not craving things of this world which we actually do not need. God is concerned about our needs because He loves us and wants to supply those needs.

In Philippians, Paul talks about the joy of giving, and then proceeds to tell how he has learned to live in both plenty and poverty. In verse 17 he explains that the greatest joy he received from their gift was knowing that the Philippians would be blessed because they gave.

In 1 Corinthians, Paul encourages the Christians in Corinth to give in an organized manner, a certain amount for a specific gift on a regular, weekly basis. These three Scripture passages help us sort out our feelings about what we need and what we give. It is up to the individual woman to determine through prayer and orderly thinking what she needs and what she should share. Each woman should go through the process privately and see what God leads her to do in this regard. It is not something that your friend can tell you to do since each person's needs and potentials are different.

6. *What can we learn from these passages for today's woman and her budget?*
   a. *Write down three principles you have learned about your budget and how it is related to your faith.*
      1) Realize we are in God's world
      2) Trust in God to supply our needs
      3) Care for our souls before our "barns"
      4) Seek wisdom in all things
      5) Be willing to give sacrificially to others
      6) Be honest about money
   b. *Go over your budget with these principles in mind. Make whatever changes are necessary to bring your budget under scriptural guidelines. This is truly a*

"homework" question and should entail more than just a glance at a scribbled checkbook balance. Encourage your group to seriously go over their financial situations. Each woman will have a different budget, but you may ask each of the women in your group to share one insight she has learned about budgeting. One might be: "Every time I overdraw or overspend, I am inadvertently telling my husband he is not a good provider."

APPLICATION

Our marriage counselors tell us that money problems can and do undermine many marriages. If we as women of faith have a grasp of God's principles about money, we are a long way down the road toward a good understanding of the family budget, as well as many other areas of finance. Our problems usually come from always wanting a little more than we currently have, and this attitude goes completely against Paul's comments on being content with that which is presently in our possession. Greed is our problem, not money.

Challenge each woman to examine her life style and budget with an eye to simplifying it, not adding to it. She may find she has more to give to others than she ever thought possible, and she will find in applying these Scriptures that God is already at work in her life giving her everything she needs.

UNIT V: FAITH THAT GROWS AND GOES

Now that your group has had some practical experience in living the life of faith, these lessons on encouragement and perseverance should be valuable. Some of the women have found themselves inadequate for certain situations. Some of them have tried the principles of faith at home or at work and been disappointed in the results. In other words, by now they have experienced some failures in trying to live the life of faith.

This unit will help your group understand that failure is not the end of the life of faith, but it is actually where they will begin to realize the full value of their faith. Faith should not be set aside when things go wrong; rather it can be the lighthouse during the storm, or the strong foundation when the house begins to shift. The fact that there is a reliable and loving Person to go to with one's problems is what Christianity is all about. Peter's words, "Cast all your anxiety on him because he cares for you" (1 Peter 5:7), come alive when for the first time a distraught woman gives her failure to a loving, heavenly Father.

By learning the appropriate balance between faith and failure, and by studying the life of Mary, the stage is set for further growth in the Christian life. The glimpses we have of Mary show us a woman of concern, devotion, and grief. The example she provides as she grows and goes on in her faith will be a constant encouragement to the group you are leading. This unit is meant to be a time of joyfully sharing within your group God's program of maturing through trials.

11

YOU AND FAILURE: "HERE I GO AGAIN"

As Christian women we have all the necessary equipment for leading a life of growth in Christ. We are forgiven; we are confident about the future because of God's promises; and we can have daily fellowship with God and other Christians. But things do not always turn out right. We still sin and have problems. Does this mean we are failing or that God is failing us? What does the Bible say in regard to these questions?

As the leader of your group, you need to explain the pattern of failure and forgiveness, temptation and victory. Probably your honest acknowledgment of these processes in your life will be a valuable testimony to the others. God's most useful servants and most productive witnesses are *all* subject to failure because they are human; so we should not become alarmed when we see ourselves falling short. What we do need to know is what to do when failure occurs, and how to turn our guilt into God's victory.

The keys to victory are in the Scriptures mentioned in this

lesson, and by now everyone in your group should have realized by experience her need for the right keys. Our goal is to appropriate God's forgiveness instead of operating continually under the guilt of failure.

PURPOSE

To understand that God can show His power through our failures.

OUTLINE

   I. Two outlooks on failure
      A. Paul's (2 Cor. 4:7—5:5)
      B. God's (Ps. 103)

  II. Two reasons for failure
      A. The old nature (Rom. 7;8)
      B. The spiritual warfare (Eph. 6:12,13)

 III. Two purposes for failure
      A. Discipline (Heb. 12:3-11)
      B. Patience (James 1:2-4)

  IV. Two solutions for failure
      A. Forgiveness (Rom. 6:23; 1 John 1:9)
      B. Prevention (Eph. 6:10-18)

   V. Two principles about failure
      A. God's victory (John 16:33)
      B. Our victory (Rom. 8:37-39; 1 Cor. 10:13)

KEY VERSES

"No, in all these things we are more than conquerors through him who loved us. For I am convinced that neither death nor life, neither angels nor demons, neither the present nor the future, nor any powers, neither height nor depth, nor anything else in all creation, will be able to separate us from the love of God that is in Christ Jesus our Lord" (Rom. 8:37-39).

"No temptation has seized you except what is common to man. And God is faithful; he will not let you be tempted beyond what you can bear. But when you are tempted, he will also provide a way out so that you can stand up under it" (1 Cor. 10:13).

"I have told you these things, so that in me you may have peace. In this world you will have trouble. But take heart! I have overcome the world" (John 16:33).

ANSWERS TO QUESTIONS

1. *Often we think our problems are unique, but each one of us has problem areas. How did a man like Paul cope with problems and failure? Read 2 Corinthians 4:7–5:5.* Paul accepted the fact that he was human and would not always have an easy life. 1) He was convinced that any problems he had existed so that God's power could be revealed. 2) He realized that our difficulties are chances to show Christ to our friends. 3) He looked forward to heaven when he would be released from his earthly body. 4) He knew that his inner strength was growing.

2. *Read Psalm 103; Romans 6:23; and 1 John 1:9. What is God's attitude toward our problems and failures?* God is merciful toward us and never tries to balance our failures with punishment. He knows that we are human and will fail. His love constantly surrounds those who reverence Him. He knows that we sin, but He has set up the provision for confession and forgiveness to protect us from carrying the guilt of our sins for a lifetime.

3. *What do the following verses have to say about failure? What is the purpose in failure?*

    a. *Hebrews 12:3-11:* It may be that God is trying to show us an area of our life which does not please him. Discipline may be simply "getting our attention" by some means or another. Discipline here refers more to the teaching (rather than the physical) aspects of punishment.

    b. *James 1:2-4:* Do not try to always avoid problems, because through them our patience has a chance to grow and perseverance can develop.

4. *Why do we fail from time to time?*

    a. *Romans 7:18-25.* Our old nature still conflicts with our new nature, but we are not slaves to the old since Jesus has set us free. (See also Rom. 8:1-4.)

    b. *Ephesians 6:12,13.* We are in the midst of a spiritual warfare and some of our difficulties come as a result of this conflict.

5. *If "an ounce of prevention is worth a pound of cure," what can you do to prepare yourself for possible hard times or failure? Read Ephesians 6:10-18 and list the preventions mentioned.*

    1) Remember God's strength.
    2) Put on God's armor.
    3) Put on the belt of truth.
    4) Use the breastplate of righteous approval.
    5) Wear the shoes of preaching the gospel of peace.
    6) Carry the shield of faith.
    7) Wear the helmet of salvation.
    8) Carry the sword of the Spirit — the Word of God.
    9) Pray constantly.
    10) Be alert.

6. *To be sure that you have the "sword of the Spirit" with you, memorize the following verses: Romans 8:37-39; 1 Cor. 10:13; and John 16:33.* Encourage your women to actively

employ these verses in their lives the next time they see a failure at their doorstep. They may not be able to avoid the failure, but now through faith they will be able to stand the test as God's women in the midst of the problem; and now they know that God walks with them through anything that may happen in their lives. Psalm 23:4 is another excellent verse to memorize in connection with this lesson.

APPLICATION

All too often Christians live with the mistaken idea that someday everything will be different and we will no longer have problems and failures. Through this study your group has learned that this mistaken idea is certainly not going to be the case for believers. The Word of God warns us that problems will occur and then goes on to help us prepare ourselves to face problems with God's solutions and spiritual armor. We are now able to recognize the fact that our world is full of problems and that we will continue to have them as Christians; however, we now have solutions and a Companion that others can never know unless they too adopt a faithful attitude toward Christ. Encourage the women in your group to actively apply the scriptural principles about failure to their own lives and to begin to live joyfully because God goes before them into the successes and failures of each day. And on the other side of the coin, sometimes the successes can be just as hard to handle without God's help as the failures. We must allow God, not our ego, to gather the trophies; and we must allow God, not the world, to heal our wounds.

12

YOU AND FAITH THAT GROWS:
A STEP AT A TIME

Through the eyes of Mary, you and your group will look at the experiences of a woman whose life was unique in many ways. On closer study, we see that she had to cope with the basics of life as well as the miraculous. As Christian women we need to know about both of these areas, the routine as well as the miracles of being a wife and mother. As we reach into Mary's life for information about faith, we see examples from her experiences and emotions. She was sometimes puzzled, sometimes confident, sometimes joyful, and sometimes heartbroken about her Son.

Our faith grows through life's experiences in different ways than Mary's, but only because God has different blueprints for our lives than He had for hers. Encourage your class to become involved in discovering the spiritual secrets that Mary has to share with us. Her life may have been different, but her equipment is exactly the same that God offers to us in the twentieth century.

Probably you will find that the women in your class are unwilling to disband when you reach this final lesson. The concerns and joys that have been shared have hopefully built a circle of friends who will want to continue to grow as Christians together. Now it will be your joy to suggest another topic of study and to go on to a deeper knowledge of the Scriptures together.

Since the growth of Christians in this life is never really over, we need the constant renewal of our faith to meet the challenges of each new day with the ever-fresh Word of God.

PURPOSE

To understand the lifelong principle of spiritual growth.

OUTLINE

I. Mary: A woman of praise (Luke 1)
   A. Her willing heart (v. 38)
   B. Her song of praise (vv. 46-55)

II. Mary: a woman of faith
   A. Her promised Son (Luke 2:13-23)
   B. Her practical faith (John 2:1-12)

III. Mary: a woman of pain
   A. Her presence at the cross (John 19:25-27)
   B. Her need for care (John 19:26)

IV. Mary: a woman of obedience.
   A. Her willingness to bear the Savior (Luke 1:38)
   B. Her trust in her son: "Do whatever He says" (John 2:1-11)
   C. Her obedience to her son's command: Live with John (John 19:25-27)

KEY VERSES

"And Mary said: 'My soul praises the Lord and my spirit

rejoices in God my Savior, . . . for the Mighty One has done great things for me — holy is his name' " (Luke 1:46,47,49).

ANSWERS TO QUESTIONS

1. *Read Luke 1:26-56.*
    a. *What characteristic of faith is seen in Mary in verse 38?* In this verse, Mary reveals to God her willingness to do whatever He has planned for her. She wants everything to happen that God has proposed.
    b. *What characteristic is seen in Mary in verses 46 and 47?* In these verses we get a glimpse of Mary's attitude toward God — one of worship and praise. She also acknowledges Him as her Savior and this is before the birth of Jesus.
    c. *Put Mary's song of praise (vv. 46-55) into your own words.*

    I cannot help but praise the Lord;
    I must rejoice that He is my Savior.
    Why should He take notice of me, a young girl?
    Why should I be the one to be honored by future generations?
    Well, . . . I don't know the answer, but He does.
    For some reason He has done a great thing through me!
    I just hope that other generations will see this.

    His mercy reaches them just like it did me;
    Then they will praise Him just like I do!
    Just look at Him. . . .

    He is so powerful that He can scatter proud, strong men.
    He is able to dethrone princes and raise up lowly humans.
    He will fill those who bring their emptiness to Him.

He will send emptiness to those who fill their lives
with anything other than Him.
Don't forget how much He has helped Israel,
And let us look forward to how He will keep all those
promises to Abraham.
This is the kind of mercy I sang about before —
mercy that goes on from generation to generation,
mercy that is eternal.

d. *Write your own song of praise.*

Each part of what is written to answer this question
should be a personal revelation of the now-woman's
relationship with God. Now that she knows something
about walking step-by-step with God, she should be
encouraged to write it down and share it with the other
members of the group. It will be rare if every woman in
your group writes something, but it will help the other
women vocalize what they are feeling about walking
with God on a daily basis. Encourage everyone to write
something, no matter how brief.

If several good poems or songs are written, you might
want to have these typed up for all of the members of the
class to have. If so, why not include some of the recipes
for faith that came out of lesson 4.

2. *What sort of life did Mary have?*

a. *Luke 2:13-23.* Mary quietly thought about what God
was doing in her life and in the life of her young son.
Surely she heard about the heavenly choir and the host
of heaven which appeared to the shepherds. Mary and
Joseph carefully kept the Jewish laws of their day: the
baby was circumcised; Mary went to the temple for
purification; and the baby was taken to Jerusalem to be
presented to the Lord. Except for her unusual devotion
and conception, Mary was like any ordinary Jewish girl.

b. *John 2:1-12*. In this passage we catch a glimpse of Mary and Jesus functioning as part of the family unit. They were attending a wedding when the wine ran out. Apparently Mary had some knowledge that Jesus could help the situation because she came to Him with the dilemma. With a word or two to those around, Mary set the stage for what has been called Jesus' first public miracle. It is recorded that soon afterward He left to spend a few days with His family. So we see Mary as very much a part of her community and quite involved in her son's life.

c. *John 19:25-27*. At the crucifixion of her son, Mary is seen by Jesus and "given" to John as a responsibility. In the days when there was no welfare or charity, this arrangement was essential for Mary's well-being in her later years.

In these three passages we see parts of Mary's life. Surely her heart broke when she saw Jesus hanging on the cross, the same one who had been heralded by the angels and who had rescued the ill-planned wedding party. She had shared in both the preparation for and the final hour of the Savior.

d. *Acts 2*. Mary faithfully waits with the other disciples for the promise of the Spirit. She had shared in her Son's resurrection and knew the life they had shared truly was victorious, even though the cross must have broken her heart.

3. *Review question 6 of lesson 1. Has any progress toward accomplishing this characteristic been seen in your life? Tell your prayer partner or your leader the answer to this question when the group meets.* Many times God changes us without our even realizing that the change has been made; but sometimes the process of change is rather painful. The women in your group will be able to share in this

question how the process of change has worked in their lives. The desired characteristic may not have been unattainable after all. Or perhaps in praying about it, the characteristic was realized as one that did not suit the woman who was wishing for it, and God in His kindness has in some way revealed that to her.

4. a. Write a description of the woman of faith as you see her. Use Mary and the other women studied as your guide.

   b. Contrast yourself as a woman of faith with these women. Tell specifically how the Workshop on Faith has been used in your life.

This question allows for evaluation of the impact of the lessons you have led. Through answering this question, your class will see that they have learned, grown, and progressed over the past several weeks. Sharing of ideas and blessings at the end of this lesson should be the showcase of how God works and should set the stage for your next study together.

APPLICATION

The lesson in this chapter is simple: Reach out for a similar attitude. God does not need another to be the mother of the Savior, but He will put us to work for Himself in ways that will specially lend themselves to our talents and abilities, just as Mary was suited for her role in special ways.

In reaching the end of this course of study, you may want to take some time to review the basic thoughts from each lesson. This will also be an excellent time for the women of the class to share some of their experiences in trying to apply the scriptural teachings they have learned.

Again, as a creative leader and hostess there are several "endings" you can put on this course. Perhaps this would be an opportunity to have a couples' dinner party at one of the larger homes in your group. This could be a time for just dinner and informal sharing and fun, or perhaps you could bring in a program or a speaker who would particularly appeal to the men. Ask God to lead you to the right kind of finale for your group, and expect that He will put on just the finishing touch that it needs.

SUGGESTED READING LIST

WOMEN'S RESOURCE BOOKS

Dobson, James. *What Wives Wish Their Husbands Knew About Women.* Wheaton, IL: Tyndale, 1975.

Hendricks, Howard G. *Heaven Help the Home!* Wheaton, IL: Victor Books/Scripture Press, 1974.

Howard, Tom. *Splendor in the Ordinary.* Wheaton, IL: Tyndale, 1976.

Karssen, Glen. *Her Name Is Woman.* Colorado Springs, CO: NavPress, 1976.

LaHaye, Tim and Beverly. *The Act of Marriage.* Grand Rapids, MI: Zondervan, 1976.

Lockyer, Herbert. *All the Women of the Bible.* Grand Rapids, MI: Zondervan, 1967.

Osborne, Cecil. *The Art of Understanding Your Mate.* Grand Rapids, MI: Zondervan, 1970.

———. *The Art of Understanding Yourself.* Grand Rapids, MI: Zondervan, 1967.

Price, Eugenia. *The Unique World of Women.* Grand Rapids, MI: Zondervan, 1969.

Stedman, Ray. *Family Life*. Waco, TX: Word, 1976.
Young, Amy Ross. *It Only Hurts Between Paydays*. Denver: Accent Books, 1975.

HELPFUL REFERENCE TOOLS

Davidson, F. *The New Bible Commentary*. Grand Rapids, MI: Eerdmans, 1956, 1970.
Douglas, J. D., ed. *The New Bible Dictionary*. Grand Rapids, MI: Eerdmans, 1962.
Halley, Henry E. *Halley's Bible Handbook*. Grand Rapids, MI: Zondervan, 1927, 1965.
Henry, Matthew. *Commentary on the Whole Bible*. Grand Rapids, MI: Zondervan, 1961.
Howard, Walden, ed. *Groups That Work*. Grand Rapids, MI: Zondervan, 1967.
Lum, Ada. *How to Begin an Evangelistic Bible Study*. Downers Grove, Il: Inter-Varsity Press, 1971.
Nyquist, James F. *Leading Bible Discussions*. Downers Grove, IL: Inter-Varsity, 1967.
Tenney, Merrill C. *The Zondervan Pictorial Bible Dictionary*. Grand Rapids, MI: Zondervan, 1967.
Unger, Merrill. *Unger's Bible Handbook*. Chicago: Moody, 1957.
Viening, Edward. *The Zondervan Topical Bible*. Grand Rapids, MI: Zondervan, 1969.
Zondervan Expanded Concordance. Grand Rapids, MI: Zondervan, 1968.